REARRANGEMENT OF THE INVISIBLE

REARRANGEMENT OF THE INVISIBLE

GAIL RUDD ENTREKIN

POETIC MATRIX PRESS

Other books by Gail Rudd Entrekin

Change (will do you good) (Poetic Matrix Press, 2005)
You Notice the Body (Hip Pocket Press, 1998)
John Danced (Berkeley Poets Workshop & Press, 1983)

Cover photo of Mt. Shasta by author

Copyright © 2012 by Gail Rudd Entrekin

ISBN: 978-0-9852883-5-8

All rights reserved. No part of this book may be used or reproduced in any manner whatsoever without written permission, except in the case of quotes for personal use and brief quotations embodied in critical articles or reviews.

Poetic Matrix Press
www.poeticmatrix.com

*For all of us grown-up children.
Imagine our surprise.*

Thanks to Molly Fisk and Madeline Tiger for their invaluable critiques of this manuscript.

Poems from this collection have previously appeared in the following publications: *After Shocks: The Poetry of Recovery for Life-Shattering Events* (Santa Lucia Books), Again!, *More Hot Flashes* (Left Coast Writers), California Quarterly, Canary, Cimarron Review, *Conversations* (Rattlesnake Interview Series), *Cradle Songs: An Anthology on Motherhood* (Quill & Parchment Press), Crazy Child Scribbler, Dogwood, Earth's Daughters, Echoes, Eclipse, Gift of Love Poetry Project (CD), Glass, Green Hills Literary Lantern, *Hot Flashes* (Left Coast Writers), Levure Litteraire (France), Lily Literary Review, *The Long and Winding Road* (Dzanc Books), *Love Over 60: 100 Women Poets Over 60* (Blackhawk Press), *Love Over 60: An Anthology of Women's Poetry* (Mayapple Press), Main Street Rag, Manorborn, *Manzanita: Poetry and Prose of the Mother Lode and Sierra*, Newport Review, Nevada County Arts Council: Women's Writing Salon, Nimrod International Journal, *Panik: Candid Stories of Life Altering Experiences Surrounding Pregnancy* (Lulu Press), Persimmon Tree, poemaday.com, Poetic Matrix, poetryrepairs.com, Sacramento Guide to the Arts, *San Diego Poetry Annual 2009-10* (Garden Oak Press), Snail Mail Review, Spillway, Sugar Mule, Theodate, The Toucan, *Turning a Train of Thought Upside Down* (Scarlet Tanager Press).

Awards:
Finalist for the Violet Reed Haas Poetry Contest from Snake Nation Press, 2011
Finalist for the Pablo Neruda Prize from Nimrod International Journal, 2011
Western States Award, Persimmon Tree, 2011

Contents

Gone with the River
- Longing 5
- Chemo 7
- Recovery Room 8
- 14 Ways of Looking at the Diagnosis 10
- Cracks 13
- Edinburgh 14
- Fear 15
- Rearrangement of the Invisible 17

My Silver Hand on You
- Shaving Our Heads 21
- The Monk 22
- Making the Bed 23
- Figure-Ground Exercise 24
- Mexico 25
- The Benefit of Dreaming 27
- Worry 29
- My Brief Experiment in Magical Thinking 31
- Hammock (Week 14, Chemotherapy) 32
- Thanks Giving 33
- Chronic Lymphocytic Leukemia 34
- Tree Frogs 35

Suppose a Mother
- The System 39
- Setting Out 40
- The Ghost in the House 41
- The Door 42

  Letting Go 43
  The Hole in the House 44
  Deciding 45
  Longer Days 46
  Not Going Back 47
  The Christmas Ball 49
  Katy's Radiator 51
  Celebration and Lament 52
  Spring Break 53

Secret Arrows

  Fame 57
  Touch 59
  The One Night Stand 61
  Waterworks Restaurant 62
  Little Animal 63
  When You Were a Boy................................. 64
  The Plant Has a Moment of Self-Awareness 65
  Creation... 67
  Prom Queen 68

Spilled Honey

  Broken (A Rant)... 71
  The Answer 72
  The Drought, the Famine, the Vulture............. 73
  Watching... 74
  What the Fortune Teller Doesn't Say 75
  Life After 76
  End Game 78
  Honesty... 79

AFTER 81
DAYLIGHTING STRAWBERRY CREEK 83
COMING HOME 84
SOMETHING COMING 85
YOU NOTICE THE BODY: REPRISE 86
THE OTHER BODY 88
THE TRAIN 90

BIOGRAPHY

Rearrangement of the Invisible

Gone with the River

Longing

is for more of this moment:
your breath in my hair,
you sleeping replete, my hand
so careful on your tender ribs
where the pain, your poor lung
like a small wet pillow

how they sucked it flaccid & deflated,
shoved it aside while they cut & siphoned,
chest tube thwacking away in dark,
then blew it all back in & pumped
it up, glued up those slits in your rising
and falling abdomen

                        here
where your shaved hair blossoms
its new delicate filaments
under my fingers — longing
for you even now when I have you —
your breath stuttering in its new way,
a rest and then a fast hard pull,
the lung, that kidney bean, still
wringing itself out like an overloaded
sponge.

           Dreamer — your poem last night
about the man who found his dream
and lost it, the miner who threw back
the biggest nugget without looking
at it until it was gone with the river —

Keep me with you now
attached to your side like

a Siamese twin. Take me
with you when you go —
This is my longing:
never to breathe
a single breath
in a world without you in it
dreaming.

CHEMO

There was a blank spot in the yard
hard-packed earth beside the chicken coop
partly shaded by oaks — I asked the man
to build a box wide and tall, where I could
sink my hands in soil without bending
all the way to the ground.
If I plant, he will live.

I am making a garden, carrots from seed,
starter tomatoes: Sun Gold and Early Girl,
baby broccolis called Munchkins (bought mainly
for the name), lemon cucumbers, zucchinis, basil
for pesto, and glads for, well, gladnesss.

                                        I'm planting
those dried brown husks of tubers, hoping
for brilliant pinks and oranges, heavy-headed
dahlias that slip out of the earth and burst into bloom
just when you'd forgotten where you put them,
given up watching. I'm filling the box with way
too much green and growing, spreading my risk
around, tending carefully, pinching out carrot
seedlings where they're too crowded and can't
survive, my metal trowel digging and moving
the struggling cucumbers out from under
the broad leaves of the muscular zucchinis,
tenderly watering the tiny clumps of sweet
alyssum around the edges, my back
against the tall deer fence
that's keeping them all
safe.

Recovery Room

A cheerful nurse has come for me
to say that you are waking
and she leads me through the swinging door
into a room with three cream-colored mummies
lined up on their cots, and the farthest one,
unquestionably, is you, my boney balding
silver-bearded angel, just returning
from your flight, your dream sleep
someplace where no tubes and wires
pin you to this world,
no machines swallow you up,
take pictures of your organs,
find out things about you
that you don't know yourself,
no men cut and paste and fail
to tell you what they know
and we, so desperately, need
to know.

      The blue of your eyes
is the only color in the face of your absence,
and for a long time you drift in and out
so it's hard to know when you are here.
But now you part your dry lips, search
for your voice, and ask again, *What did he say?*
I tell you again, unfazed by this repetition,
not so very different from our daily forgettings,
our system of gentle reminders, learning
to set aside our pride, our touchiness,
to laugh because sorrow is so wearing.

I take your long cold hand in my two
warm ones as I have taken you again
and again into my heat, and I tell you,
We have to wait and see.

14 Ways of Looking at the Diagnosis

1.
In the waiting room,
filling out forms.
Someone has hand-written in pencil
under diagnosis: *leukemia*.

2.
She sobs every morning
the second he closes the door.
She understands, as he doesn't yet,
that it's never going to be the same again.

3.
For a long time he believes
it's a mistake.

4.
She emails all the kids.
They come homing in a flock,
incredulous and stunned.

5.
She searches his body
for new signs. She stares at the swelling
on the side of his face, almost
licks it.

6.
He tells her he dreamt she told him
they should divorce now
so the children get used to
not having him around
before he dies.

7.
She looks up statistics on the Internet,
acquaints herself with worst case scenarios,
imagines waking up alone in their bed.

8.
He becomes timid, begins
to think of himself
as a dying man.

9.
He shaves off his 40-year-beard,
says he wants to see
himself one more time –
is shocked to find
an old man.

10.
After a couple of months
he wakes up from the long
slow trance. He says
he plans to live.

11.
He stops her in the kitchen,
takes her shoulders in his hands,
says he's glad it's him
instead of her. She says
she wishes they could share it,
each be only half as sick.

12.
They plan to simplify their life
in case he becomes unable to help.
She says she hates
their unique life
becoming a cliché.

13.
When they make love
she weeps, is sorry for
ruining the present
by grieving the future.

14.
They don't know how it will end,
but everybody dies.

CRACKS

Mostly I notice the cracks:
the way it didn't look when I
brought it home, how things break down,
often aided by children and animals,
a perfect vase and twelve years later
I notice the hairline where it's been glued.
The child itself, a round pink creature
100 percent whole and with a 360-degree future
begins to flaw and flake, gets spots, doesn't do well
at math, requires an insulin pump, and the ceiling
starts to tremble, the chandeliers swing.

I need to sleep in the arms
of a deep cradle in a familiar night
where everything returns to the fullness
of nothing-happened-yet – safety in stasis –
this changing so full of rocky outcroppings
cliff slides and mud, small thuds in the night.

Edinburgh

Caught in the net of your illness
with its fibers of fear, as we walked
the cobblestones in Edinburgh,
the rainy steps, you slowed down,
held back, an almost immovable presence
behind us, making us step and again wait
when all that was bright,
all the colors, shops with their baskets
of woolen scarves, men in kilts with feathers
in their caps, piping in the streets, tourists
in their Uggs and awkward raincoats,
were all around us: movement, sound, color.

We wanted to see it all: the heather
and the misty grey green hills of Aberdeen
and Inverness, the lochs of music and myth,
spread below us, the isles of strange and lonely birds.

We couldn't feel your eyes aching. We kept forgetting
how inside your head there were clouds, a smudged lens,
and you couldn't get your bearings, left us to struggle with maps,
find the Starbucks and the castle. You left us in charge
by default, and we didn't want the job, wanted you back
leading on in your striped red scarf, your Scottish cap,
your firm and certain compass showing the way, your smile,
clear-eyed, familiar.

FEAR

Fear tastes like pennies, sounds like
that shush when you clasp your hands
over your ears, float below the surface of the pool
where there are voices on TV, birds, cars arriving,
but you can't make any of it out.
The brain's red alert shuts out all interference;
they could be behind your back now
revoking your right to speak, poisoning your water,
torturing your neighbor, and it would come to you
as a faint annoyance because the thing,
the thing that might happen, has sucked
all the air from the room and you are
focusing the high beam of your mind
on survival.
                If you fall into snakes
in the dark there is horror, which is separate
from fear, and if you need a doctor but you can't pay
there is panic, also a separate thing. They know
fear is the thing you can't see,
and they use it,
the thing waiting
around the next bend in the road,
when the brain's messages are
stacking up behind each other,
running into each other like cars
in a freeway pile-up, and they keep you
on Yellow Alert so you'll focus,
ignore the man behind the curtain,
the one manipulating the life of your son
with strings and mirrors. What is it?
What should we watch for?
It might be a terrorist bomb
ticking in a shoe,

an unusually hot autumn,
the disappearance of frogs.
It might be everything;
it might be nothing at all.

Rearrangement of the Invisible

And here he comes again, that querulous old man
with his pointy hat, his knobby walking stick,
curl-toed shoes, pulling behind him the next installment
of your life, whether you're ready or not,
sweeping ahead in his push broom the scraps
and shards of your story so far —

Just as you were getting used to the white roses,
those blowsy blooms along the edges of the lawn,
the doe steps delicately out of the dark
while you're sleeping, incises every bud,
every blossom, leaving naked sticks piercing
the night, and despite the dog throwing herself
against the door, by the time you push it open,
stagger out in your threadbare nightshirt,
the deer has slipped away like a ghost
into the woods beyond the pointless fence.

You wake in the morning to a whole new landscape,
and when you cry out, wringing your hands and cursing,
the dog sits down and fixes you in her patient gaze —
she tried to tell you (but you wouldn't wake up)
that the old man was passing down the road
rearranging your future, and the thing growing
in your bones, which won't be identified for weeks,
is the seed of a whole new order.

My Silver Hand on You

Shaving Our Heads

I say I'll shave my head, become a moon-
face bald pink shining defenseless-
seeming creature in some kind of funny hat,

when your hair falls out in tufts on the pillow case
in the morning, your crisp silver beard thins,
soft flesh under chin shows through.

When we shave our hair, our skin-covered skulls,
which we have never seen, will be revealed,
embarrassed in their naked whiteness,

their lumps and bumps and funny spots, no help
for the unfortunate contours of our faces,
our strange prominent nose or ears,

heads that haven't been seen by anyone
since we were babies and our mothers
ran their fingers through our delicate fuzz,

our fathers palmed our noggins
in their callused hands, admired how like
heavy fruit we felt, and wondered who was waiting
inside these perfect structures,
these elegant bony domes.

THE MONK

Zipping out our road this morning
in my green Beetle, up ahead,
along the shoulder in the steam of sun,
there materialized a monk in saffron
and scarlet robes, shaved head,
walking away from me. As I passed
I turned back to see his face.
I must have looked ... surprised, delighted
intrigued ... I was all those things –
the mystery of his presence there –
a Tibetan monk on Wet Hill Road
beside a row of cedars, talking
on a cell phone.

I drove to the gym, lifted weights,
did yoga, took a shower, still
in the glow of that moment, so that
turning onto my road, heading home,
I was not even surprised to see him again
miles up the road from our earlier passing,
this time heading toward me, no phone
but what looked like fat yellow ear muffs
or head phones, and as I passed
he lifted his hand, met my eyes,
smiled with delight as though,
exactly as though, we had scheduled
this meeting, had been coming toward
each other from two distant places
all our lives.

Making the Bed

I'd like to tear those petals with my teeth
the deer keep eating roses when I call
them lovely
              I call you lovely   I mustn't
bite down   though your body pushes into me
I can tuck you into my flesh   I can keep you safe
I cannot keep you safe   consuming you
I'm only one more aberrant organism taking
over your cells   I'd like to also eat this purple
eggplant before the deer get to it
                                      you
I'd like to hide your hands in the folds
of my flannel pocket   bend down and let me
lick your eyes   here your wounds are   healing
and scabbing   let me   don't let me   make
you small   soft and blue
                                  put you down my dress
where no one sees   keep my silver hand on you
all day   wherever I run

Figure-Ground Exercise

Some days we dream
and weep cancer, talk and write it,
carry it with us to the grocery store,
propped up in the back seat like a gaunt old man.
We put cancer in a high chair and feed it
scraps from the table, nominate cancer
for president because it is even handed
and blind. We find cancer all over
our hands when we wake in the morning
and we cannot scrub it away; we kiss it goodnight
when we turn to each other, put out the light.
We see cancer in the center of the drawing,
a curving vase, the rest of our lives
twin shadows on either side.
      Better days
we cannot remember the word from our dreams
and once we get busy, it disappears.
There are pink roses outside the front window,
geese honking on their way to Puerta Vallarta
where they plan to gamble and drink green liqueur.
Our cold toes poke each other playfully under the covers,
grandchildren stagger about on newly vertical legs,
and the rain plashes softly around the cradle of our sleep.
In the drawing we see two matching silhouettes
facing each other with abiding interest,
the shape between them
nothing but shadow
dark air.

Mexico

In Mexico, the stomach rebels in small ways
unrelated to Montezuma or fish washed in well water.
It happens long before any specific event
or figment can trigger it, sometimes even
on the plane over those black deserted
crags, vistas of brush and dirt heaped in pointed
cones of desolation finally yielding to the luminous green
patches like mirages, a landscape dotted with false hopes,
resorts and charming villages painted by an optimistic
child in one corner of this ugly canvas
where you could perish in dust,
never be found.

                It's the total unfamiliarity,
the unwelcome, the wall of heat you can barely permeate
as you descend the metal stairway to the tarmac,
clutching your straw hat, the sun unleashed by the thin
indifferent atmosphere – the veiled or imagined hostility
in the eyes of the dark-skinned worker,
his dirty blue jumpsuit like a prison uniform,
a third world bandana tied around his head.

You have come to play and you are willing
to pay for your fun, will slide those 20-peso
notes into the brown hands of drivers,
bellmen, waiters, and tell yourself
this is their job. But when you ask,
the driver tells you he never takes vacations,
never goes away. They never stop doing
what they do for you, whenever you
wish to spend.

That brown worm
curled at the bottom of the Cuervo
has entered your belly like a dark night
and the first pain is telling you
there will be hell to pay.

The Benefit of Dreaming
for Denny

I hope this is a dream. My brother is cutting wood in the yard
at his old farmhouse, the one he sold after his divorce
20 years ago, and the power saw he's holding slides
along the branch, slits his jeans, bores into the white flesh
of his thigh in the time it takes him to gasp.
He stands and we all stare at the color sinking
out of his ruddy face, collecting somewhere in his body
and appearing all at once at the tear in his pants,
welling up in a long line before he drops
to one knee, shaking.

                      But isn't this real? Don't two
or three of us spend the whole afternoon and evening
at the ER in Lancaster, watching farmers with severed digits
and old men with heart attacks carried into the inner
sanctum? Don't we wait and wait and wait, my brother holding
his leg together, lowering his head now and then to avoid fainting,
until finally they sew the tendon end-to-end and we all go home?

In another dream or memory, my brother and I sit on dirty
orange shag carpet in his living room – no furniture –
no food in the fridge – nothing but beer. We lean
against the wall of this last chance apartment and both of us
are crying. We look to be in our twenties, yet already each
of us has failed at something we really wanted: law school,
marriage. At least we are a little drunk.

If there is some important secret our parents
forgot to impart, some family curse we are swimming in,
at least for tonight we are swimming in it together.
This is the benefit of dreaming.

Doesn't he call to tell me
from 3000 miles away that though we thought things could never
get worse, though in fact things got a lot better and stayed that way
for years and years, now they are decidedly collapsing around him.
He has lost all his money; his wife, the very bloom of his heart,
is leaving him and taking the little boys whose growth sustains him;
and he has just come from the hospital where they looked grave,
murmured *insulin, needles, blood pressure,*
pills, ulcers, pain. And then he saw that
for all of this he cannot pay.

In this dream I tell him
that I too am waiting, listening to the word *lymphoma* repeat
itself again and again in the discordant music of my nights. And though
we don't cry, holding our phones, looking out on opposite oceans,
we confess how we do weep suddenly in our car or shower,
how this breaking is a small and puzzling comfort.

Worry

The dogs, those big lugs who squeezed
past my knees at the door a week ago,
are running in the morning, all out, in spite of the older dog's
hips, his bad knee, they are arcing over a golden field
leaping and settling and leaping like undersized deer
and now they have come to a trail. They settle
to a steady lope, come up short at a grove
of elder trees to stop and sniff, pick up mountain
lion, and they both hunch down, noses to ground,
ease forward cautiously, heads lifted now to check the breeze,
quivering, and finally they stop. Danger danger danger.
But the lion on the hill just above the path doesn't pounce,
though maybe she could take the limping dog down,
doesn't want to deal with the larger fresher dog,
watches the two beasts move on.

They are by the river now, picking their way over
the smooth rocks to get down to the water and drink.
Suddenly thirst is the only impulse, huge and red and swelling,
so the old dog, Smokey, goes too, though he knows he slips,
and he does slip, just as they reach the water, slides in with a
    small splash,
is carried down river fast, bumping rocks, paddling hard,
trying to get his footing, while Chloe runs along the shore,
slipping too, sliding almost in, getting her footing, scrambling
on, keeping him in her nose, and finally finds him, twisted
in a hollow, his back leg stuck between a bolder and a branch.
She pushes him, and he lifts his head, dripping and panting,
and when he doesn't get up, she lies down beside him in the sun.

Now it is evening of the fifth day. She has gone in search of help
from strangers, but though they stop to chat with her, pat her head,

they don't come down where Smokey lies. They read her tags,
offer her a ride home, but she turns away, trots back down to the river.

On the seventh day her hunger is fierce. She has eaten a dead squirrel
and some other rank thing in the woods, but the hollow in her belly
cannot be ignored. Smokey barely lifts his head when she nudges him now.
Every hour she thinks to leave him, turns to go, but always she
trots back.

        Or perhaps they burst together out of the woods
into a clearing where a ramshackle house stands, broken down cars
lie all around, and they lift their noses with joy. Chickens! They rush
across the garden, no thought for the lettuces, the delicate chard
beneath their feet, instinctively separate, Chloe heading for the far side
of the pen, Smokey stepping between the wires when suddenly there is
a blast, and he crumples to the dirt. Chloe blinks once, freezes in place,
   turns to run,
and another blast takes her down. Out there in the woods there are no
   dogs now.
No dogs running, no dogs lying together, waiting to be saved.

                 Or one dog is
caught in a trap and the other waits beside it. Or both dogs are tied
   in the yard
of a crazy man who beats and starves them. Stop.

               There are two dogs
running in the woods, the first dog's black and brown fur, long and shiny,
glints in the sun as she runs, and the old dog following her
is pushing through his pain for the sheer joy of freedom
the mindless fulfillment of doing what he's meant to do
running.

My Brief Experiment in Magical Thinking

I held my father's hand, directed
my spirit into his failing body, closed
my eyes and willed, say, half my strength
over to him, figuring with half I could make
a comeback, being young, make
new blood, new cells in my sturdy
bones, and when I looked up from my efforts,
and he was still there in his metal bed,
still dying, still staring in terror
at enormous bugs on the ceiling,
I knew, and I never forgot,
that loving him that much
was what I could do, and saving him
was what I couldn't.

Hammock (Week 14, Chemotherapy)

One of my eyes is closed against the soft fabric of your shirt,
the other open on the leafy sky, stirring and rustling
back and forth above us as we rock, your foot
on the grass, pushing off now and then
to keep us rocking.

This is the last day at the oasis before we shoulder
our cumbersome packs
and set off again onto the desert
where you will be wracked with thirst
and black dreams, and I will run beside you
urging you on, offering water from the big canteen,
reaching up to pat your forehead, fan you
with my sweaty shirt, planning what to do
if you fall and I cannot catch you – how I will
lie down in the sand and wait.

But here on the last day, under birdsong,
my skin still imprinted with your hands,
my mouth swollen with the fullness of you,
it is enough.

There will come a day
when one of us has to imagine
this moment, when what is so present
slides into the past.
We can feel time gathering now,
about to move forward.

THANKS GIVING

out of prison   we are on parole   we are getting better
two lobsters out of the pot   we are seeing the light
we are moving on   moving up   moving out
of the end of the tunnel and no train in sight
it's been dark in there   full of monstrous terrors
we were afraid   we were so afraid
and your feathers fell out all around us
we kept picking them up and tucking them in
but finally you were naked as a plucked chicken
you were lying in the pan and I was basting you
tenderly in this ointment   that oil   this basil
tarragon olive dorzolamide ratuxin chemical bath
your eyes rolled back   I could see you screaming inside
out   we got you out of the pan   trussed you up
in a new blue shirt   your hair comes back in
peachy white thin fuzz   your hands stop hurting
you stand up and walk   you remember the words
you are out   we are out here smiling

Chronic Lymphocytic Leukemia

When the monster grabbed him up, tossed him back
into its mouth, we had been swimming along holding hands
and I didn't let go, flew up dripping and dropped beside him
into the dark and foreign place where there were others
dimly swimming for their lives and there were teeth that grazed
our skins now and then as we lay very still, our hope ballooning,
rising up into the sinuses of the creature intermingled
with our fear so that both rose equally and were, we prayed,
equally compelling, but the truth, we knew, was that the beast
was dumb and barely knew we were there.
         Every day
it tested its spikes against our naked fragile bodies,
some days teasing us by tipping forward, almost letting
us roll out into the frothy sea, but most days we lay still,
read medical books, listened to the messages of friends
sending love and encouragement from far away places
where life went on in warm kitchens and the linens
were clean and dry.
      Finally, the thing decided not to decide,
let us wash out with the tide. We are swimming again
and the ocean is very blue. But there is a fin moving
beside us on the horizon, and though it disappears
from time to time in the bright sun
at dusk it is always there
circling.

TREE FROGS

There's something dark at the core
of the thing that's blowing me back,
my arms flapping like crows, but I'm making
no headway against this wind and a familiar voice
right beside me says, *Did you hear that? Is it a person?*
And my voice says, *I think it's an animal.*

But now I'm awake, the sound has changed.
The cotton it was wrapped in has fallen away.
Four a.m. and somewhere down the hill
beyond the houses and yards and trees,
maybe all the way down at the highway,
a man is yelling *Help me. For god's sake,
somebody help me.*

At the window, I am bending into the still air.
I am fumbling over 911 in the dark.
Now the voice, delirious, calls out
a long train of moan and mumble.
I envision his pain from the car
that has fallen from its jack onto his legs,
pinned him to the garage floor,
or a saw has run amuck
severed his femoral artery, some
large sharp metal thing
out here in the visible world or
the little snakes of loathing and fear
that slip through the heart's chambers,
the flopping roaches dropping from
the ceiling of the mind.

Barefoot on the cold asphalt, I find the cop's
a skinny teen-ager with a walkie-talkie and a cool flashlight.

REARRANGEMENT OF THE INVISIBLE

The minute he enters the yard, the distant voice
falls silent.
The man hanging from a nail
by his ring finger or his neck
cannot possibly last much longer
and the police have come here instead of there.

The child cop has his pal on the walkie talkie now.
They're excited, having fun. Two neighbors
on another street have also called,
he wants me to know. He tells me twice,
thinking I will be happy there has been
corroboration of my story.   But now
they will never find the man.

Someone may discover his body in a day or two.

Or he will wake up tomorrow,
uneaten, unsevered, unpoisoned after all
and see the small creatures busy in the grass
beside his bruised head
stuffy with the residue of terror.

We lie on our backs listening
into the long night. Outside
the tree frogs notice with a start
their own silence, and they take up the song
of those of us who, for the moment,
are going on.

Suppose a Mother

The System

I couldn't tell how long I left him there,
my son finally sleeping in his infant seat,
doors locked, windows cracked,
our German shepherd in back,
the van parked in front of Cody's Books
while I delivered an order.

The person in charge was out.
I had to wait; I stood at the back counter
where I couldn't keep, as I had planned,
my sick child in my line of sight, where
he dozed peacefully in his light blue
winter hat and the rain fell
and the nosey protective Berkeley
passersby gathered, the cop stood
angry, making out his report
radio in hand.

10 minutes, I said, hoping to hit
a believable number, but his mouth moved
and *irresponsible mother* and *foster care*
and *take him down to the station* hung
in the air until *you're lucky* and *I'm gonna
let you go* settled into my belly.   I was weeping
and my child slept on
                                     and my hands
shook and I remembered forever
not that my child could be kidnapped
but that I could be terrified,
shamed.

Setting Out

> "The port from which I set out
> was the port of my loneliness."
> Henry James

Isn't it always that way: the teen sobbing
on the bed, alone in the afternoon sunlight,
the dust motes from the window
where the cat sometimes sleeps,
and next door, the guy who drank
beer all night with his friends, then put
his fist through the wall in the kitchen
in a fit of rage, despair: *If there is someone
for everyone, where?* Isn't it always that parent
turning to the window saying *Don't tell me.
I don't want to know*, needing, as we do,
to preserve the image of our children
strong, confident, on a true course
to adulthood, no desperation, no critical
mistakes in the black of night
involving fast cars, muddled sex, the silver
needle shining, futures squandered
on a dusty road? Isn't it where we're all from,
the day we looked around and knew
it was time to set out from this port,
safety being not at all
enough?

THE GHOST IN THE HOUSE

Sometimes in the afternoon I see him,
blurry from sleep, silently enter the kitchen,
pour a bowl of cereal. Or just at sunset
through the door of the TV room, above the couch,
I catch a glimpse of the back of his head.
And once at three a.m. I woke to let the dog out and,
noticing light in the yard from the study windows,
I padded down the hall in my cold bare feet
and saw him there at his computer, staring.

If I say hello, he answers.

His crumpled black car appears sometimes
beside mine at the back of the driveway,
so I know he has been away and returned.

He lives here, my placid little boy who loved me.
His goatee grows from week to week,
or gets shaved away. His bedroom emits
the pale, unpleasant arc of body odor from his bedding
or the disconsolate heap of unwashed laundry.
He is thinner now. There is a case
of beer under the coffee table
that he has drunk or will drink some long night
as the house lies sleeping.

Somnambulant son: Wake up! Wake up!
My longing passes through him like sunlight.

The Door
for Ben at 24

You come in the back door in your black T-shirt,
your unplanned smile taking us both by surprise.
Quickly you recover, lean on the kitchen counter
in your dirty jeans, talk about your car, how Nick
is helping you pull the engine.
I listen, watch your mouth,
the way your face animates so briefly,
falls back into its regular mask.

But you smiled, you smiled at me. The door
of your face opened quickly and I saw inside,
how the fog stirred and lifted, showed me to you
standing in my kitchen, and I saw,
for one sweet unguarded moment,
that you were glad to see me.

Letting Go
> *for Nate*
> Sail on, silver bird. Sail on by.
> Paul Simon

My son gone today, tonight I dream him feathered:
at first small, white, frothy pinfeathers on his shoulders,
back, and upper arms, but as we hike along in the sun,
they multiply, become long, stiff, silvery white,
become smooth, silken wings with hollow spines
and long soft fronds, until he is all feathers.
I hold him to my breast to ease his fears,
and he shrinks into a little boy, his chubby legs
around my waist, and just as my joy rises up,
his little heart pounding against mine, I look down
into his yellow eyes, his cruel beak that can never
speak to me again, and feel his wings flapping
against my arms, how I've pinned them to his sides
in my embrace, and suddenly he bursts forth,
explodes through my arms out into the air.
He lifts off directly before me in a wave of feathers,
wind and beating, and I awake weeping, my face
all running and wet, and I lie there thinking the ending,
how he is soaring out over the sea,
disappearing into the sun.

The Hole in the House

Already shadows lengthen in the corners of the house
where you tend to settle: the window seat
you sleep in when the other girls are here,
the table in the corner covered in papers,
wadded dance clothes, wrinkled lunch bags,
the space you commandeered long ago and have occupied
these years. Deep in your books, methodical mind,
you sit, your back to the room, your CD player winking to the beat,
your orange cat sprawled on her back beside you on the table
soaking up heat from the burning lamp.

Already you are taking on the luminous transparency
of the leaving. You hug more quickly
and with your jacket on. You tell your stories still
but beyond me, you are glancing at the door.

Already the cat, who sleeps with you,
is pulling away in your arms, raising her head to sniff,
puzzling over something new in the air
burrowing back into your unsettled
unsettling scent.

               And I, alone in the car and feeling fine,
suddenly cry, suddenly sob because soon
there will be no chance of passing you
on the road in your silver truck,
and soon, when I walk into the house,
your blue room will boom its silence,
its emptiness, into every room
and echo down to me below, find me
standing here in sunlight,
your soft cat in my arms,
my face buried
in her winter
coat.

Deciding

Suppose a mother whose children are gone,
looking at the long straight road ahead,
feeling herself invisible and beside the point,
were to step off into the woods, leave a note
that said *I don't want to live without passion;*
could she erase herself? Could she keep blind
to the holes her betrayal would leave
in all the little boats, the way they would sink
slowly over the long years ahead, those boats
she'd made and set afloat in hope?

                                        Suppose
the woman arrives at the water and finds there
the man she has almost forgotten, waiting for her
in a kayak with red paddles. And now she gets in
the front and begins to stroke, and they pull together
in silence, dipping and turning, dipping and turning,
two figure eights in the late air, each time she raises
her paddle, the cool water trickling down along its stem
drops in shiny glints on her bare legs, and he,
without speaking, matches her stroke, controls the rudder
with his feet, steers them out onto the glittering green lake
where they see the sun drop behind the tree line, where they see
eleven ducks in a V beyond the trees in the grey pall of a fire
far away in someone else's wood, and the note she thought of writing
becomes an unremembered dream, and one lone brown straggler,
flying up from the lake beside them, calls its desperate *wait, wait*
as it lifts across the sky.

Longer Days

We try so hard to live in the new world,
the new freedom of childlessness,
the spaciousness of the empty house.
But what we're losing every day
is so much bigger than what we're gaining.

There were daily lists, toward the end,
amped up, as we were, to do the little extras
no one even asked for, both to fill
the longer days, and to do those last small
favors, the quickly-becoming-obsolete
services of love.
                    So few tasks
now, we can hold them in our heads.
And when they call we light up
like old lamps in the dusty dark.

We must stand up and go now,
make a new room, cozier,
designed for two –
a warmer place where our dimmer lights
are enough to heat us,
make our small world bright.

We must turn to each other now.
Outside it's very dark
and something we don't know
is waiting.

Not Going Back

I keep away from Indian Shack Road,
its deep curves sinking down into the granite boulders
with their iridescent green moss, the little
bundles of mistletoe hanging innocently
from the live oaks over the road,
the peacock maple that never grew, planted
in memory of Gabriel, dead at 15,
from the Granny Smith and the Gravenstein
deep rooted on the hill above the Yuba
where we climbed down to swim
and I wept climbing back up, sweating
aching and everyone else so merry; I don't go
to see the sulking seat, the chair behind the whale rock
where I hid when my children, who memory says
were always singing, were fraying and scratching
at my day.   I don't go down to the pond
where the blue gill bit our bottoms, bright red or blue
in the centers of our black inner tubes like targets
and the water iris spread along the banks in clouds
of purple — where we jumped from the redwood platform
or bounced from the mini-tramp on the lower deck
and hit the dark pond flailing.

Cherry tree: one cherry and a bird got it;
nets don't work, nor scarecrows, nor anything
on god's green earth but standing there
all day guarding it, watching it redden
in the sun.   And who has time like that
to stand and wait, breathing the first
pink blossoms espaliered on the wire fence,

watching the white tails of the deer
as they leap six feet straight up over,
disappear like mirages
into the woods?
                        Little girls' fairy houses
moss-roofed and decaying into the hillside
over there beyond the rope swing,
and down at the court with the netless rusty rim
the colored tiles my children made
imbedded in the concrete corners deep under
last year's leaves.

The new people came and everything began
to fall apart; the dam, they tell me, crumbled down the hill
and the whole pond rushed down past it to the river
that first winter while they sunned in Mexico
and shortly he took sick and died and she, unable
to either live in or sell the place in its collapse, moved
away, leaving it standing there beneath the madrones,
the little cedars we planted, now looming along the drive
above the canyon, no one stopping in the tall grass
to watch amazed a hundred geese filling the sky
with raucous song.
                      I don't go up the sledding hill
where later we built the studios, seeded with daffodils,
protected with our Celtic gods, the path the little girls beat
through the woods across the creek, threading the poison
oak between their houses – that family broken
and gone now – and strangers in the wood.

The Christmas Ball

In November with the last leaves floating
a spark ignites for the coming season,
the tabula rasa of white,
the little flashing colors,
the homing of children.

She begins the sewing of quilts and scarves,
list making, ordering of greenery,
small trips to local shops, and by December
the little ball of Christmas
is heavier, she is beginning to tire,
and chopping down the tree,
hauling it home in the truck,
she notices she's sweating now,
pushing the ball uphill alone, her husband
standing by bemused
as she types the Christmas letter,
photocopies it, writes out cards,
addresses, stamps and mails them,
hangs a wreath, climbs a tree for a clutch
of mistletoe, unpacks the candles,
the Christmas boulder growing
like a snowman under her solo power,
and when she stands it up atop the hill,
they come together laughing,
                                 unpack, eat,
unwrap, consume, break down the ball
into all its little shining pieces, exclaim
and then they go.

                       She turns,
in the failing light, begins to gather bows,
feed paper to the fire, blows out the Santa candles,

pushes up her sleeves and starts to haul away
the tree, brown and crisp, return the gifts that didn't fit,
pack up the pieces carefully so that only months
from now, fresh and forgetting, she can
begin again to roll the Christmas ball
up winter's hill.

KATY'S RADIATOR

In Glasgow the rain, a mist, tiny droplets far apart
but, in time, enough to soak our jackets, stain the toes
of our shoes dark, coils her long hair on her forehead
and cheeks. She doesn't believe in umbrellas, prides herself
on living wet, which we parents cannot be expected
to understand.

                    In the kitchen, at Kelvinhaugh Gate,
she shows us her plate, her cup, one pan, two bags of microwave
popcorn, a mini-jar of honey from a hotel, and the groceries
from the Pakistani guy in the corner store: Tetley tea, skim milk,
a peach, an apple.

                    In a room of her own, her first place,
she has a sheet, pillowcase, a blanket, a chain of little colored lights.
The windows open on grass, rain, a storage shed for bikes and suitcases.
The radiator under the window bangs and sighs.

We parents take a plane.
The image of her walking away outside the café
lingers behind our eyes,
a big strong girl with curvy hips,
swinging wet hair,
who never looked back.

Celebration and Lament

Young men, chosen almost at random,
penetrate the bodies of our daughters
and the daughters, those long-haired beauties,
enter the water in which we all have swum.

Some jump awkwardly from the wall,
arms and legs flailing, hit with a splash,
and some, like my daughter,
remove their glasses, place them carefully
on a safe ledge, slip between the waves
with surprising aplomb, sleek and easy
as porpoises skimming the blue sheets.

And all of them come up swimming,
some dog paddling till they get the hang of it,
some stroking free style in perfect rhythm,
turning their heads to take in air,
their eyes unfocused, their bodies intent
on the activity at hand.

Lined up on the cliffs,
we cannot (and should not)
really see, but we have
our own memories
of floating and sinking,
diving and rising back up
to the visible world.

SPRING BREAK

Waiting for her in the airport,
standing in the throng below the escalator
watching arriving passengers descend,
I fall into a reverie, Week 3 chemo,
and for a minute I disappear. And when
I come to, she is tapping my shoulder,
her whole face smiling, her long hair swinging
across her eyes. Her backpack on her
strong shoulders, she bends to me, smelling
the way she does, of fruit and hot sun,
and a weight inside me shifts;
I reach out for her; something black
lifts and floats away.

                      For 13 days
even if her goings are more than her comings,
even if I close my lips firmly on my mouthful of fear,
I'll open my windows to let in all her shine,
her voice will roll pleasantly over me,
bathing me in long stories, laughter,
music from another room.

Katy's home
and all the lights are on
at my house.

SECRET ARROWS

FAME

His voice felt sticky; he whispered his name,
Paulie; he saw my picture in the paper, asked
– I didn't understand the word – Did I want him
to suck something. It was something
ugly – he was a grown-up stranger –
and I didn't know how to think about it,
couldn't answer, so without even saying
good-bye I set the receiver back
on its heavy black base.

                        When my mother
came home with her arms full of brown bags
and began unpacking Miracle Whip, Oreos
and Velveeta cheese, turning back and forth
from kitchen table to cupboard to fridge,
I stood in the doorway and sailed my story
into the room, except I couldn't bring myself
to tell her what he said. Slowly, she stopped
walking, stood still and turned the beam
of her full attention on me, something
so rare that my worst fears were confirmed,
and she said maybe I'd like to tell her upstairs.

We went up to her bedroom, where the gauze curtains,
which tasted, I knew, like plastic and dust, blew
away from the bay windows that faced the street
and she closed the door and sat down on the bed.
I stood just inside the door
and forced myself to say the terrible words,
and I watched her face blanch – it must have been shocking
to hear such suggestions from a little girl with braids –
and she said yes, those were bad words indeed
and she said he was a very sick man, sick in his mind,

and she said that probably I shouldn't tell Daddy
the words he said, but she would tell him for me
and they would take care of it.

                        I felt so light,
as if I'd been carrying deadly poison
in a breakable bowl and had managed
not to drop or spill it, had safely
handed it over to someone who would
carry it up high, firmly, out of sight,
and who knew how to dispose of it
where I would never
have to see it again.

Touch

Old man, you surface seldom, singing and swaying,
stomping out the Black Bottom in the living room
in your shiny work shoes, your grey bus driver's shirt
and cap, your head thrown back, your pink Irish face
a bowl of laughter – you pressed your palm flat
to the crest of your bald dome to hold in
all that funny. Playing cards you taught me
deuce and tres. Your baritone filled the car
and rose above our mom's contralto,
my breathy soprano, my brother's clear tenor
tentative but true, swelling at the final lines:
so wait and pray each night for me
till we meet again.
                    Did you kiss
my neck when you scratched my back?
I danced on your shoes and you
taught me turn and turn and counter-turn,
to feel your partner's body move. You said,
Everything's a dance. I felt your heart.
I brushed the shining copper fur
along your muscled arms, your chest.
My mother turned away,
embarrassed. I think now,
She was not that kind of person.

When I feel my daughter's silky hair,
like liquid in my hands,
I feel you there.

                You told me not to marry
the first man who came along. You said
sample a few, make sure you like
the way they dance. Sex,

you meant. I didn't know,
this thing you saw in me,
that touch would be my world,
your touch the secret arrows
pointing the way.

THE ONE NIGHT STAND

The night I danced topless at that club in North Beach
I had walked into the bar, my last dollar in my pocket,
a torn newspaper in my hand. I had just turned 21
and my navy blue bell bottoms sat low on my hips.
I was short and curvy and my breasts were small and neat.
I couldn't pass the pencil test for big breasts, couldn't hold one
under them, but I had long dark auburn hair and I looked
like someone's little sister (I *was* someone's little sister)
and some guys like that look. I guess that's why
the silver-haired crone in pancake make-up,
looking disgusted to see me,
decided anyway to give me a go.

The cage above the bar was cold, but the music
was good: Big Pink, Janice, Iron Butterfly, and to keep
warm and kill the boredom, you really had to think
sexy thoughts, light yourself up with your own secret
lust for yourself, think of yourself with a man you'd like
to be with. It would have helped if I had had more sex
than just the one uninspired boyfriend. Imagination can
only go so far, but mine went the full eight hour shift.

By the end I was so sick of watching myself
watching myself bumping and grinding
swaying and weaving my hips,
my arms wild and winding in my hair,
my hands sliding down my hips and butt,
dreaming sexy young guys under my hands,
admiring me, begging to touch me,
trying to ignore the real life old guys in dirty jackets
who stood by the door staring for long minutes,
saying whatever it was they said and spitting.
I was inside my cage, inside my head
and no one could touch me but myself.

WATERWORKS RESTAURANT
Columbus, Ohio

We were walking fast in our long dresses
balancing our trays   we were singing along
with The Eagles   bouncing in rhythm   serving
plates of steaks   chatting with celebrating groups
whose team   Ohio State   had won the day
and who would later leave us 20-dollar bills
we were stopping in the pantry to eat the "spit-backs"
that hadn't been touched   the apple pie
stuffed-baked potato with sour crèam & chives
teriyaki chicken   we were pinching bottoms
being pinched   laughing   calling out orders to Rick
or Craig behind the bar in his funny apron and
we were moving fast and happy   we were very
very good at what we did and we
were young and we
were only passing through.

Little Animal

The small tame animal of you, blind,
dependent on touch,
nuzzles my thigh, my hand, my face,
seeking in the way an infant,
held to anyone's chest,
will turn his face, press into fabric,
pushing it aside, smelling for milky flesh,
the way a dog you love
will use its face to find you,
its nose to your skin
like a tiny vacuum cleaner
sucking up the story of where you've been
and what you have to offer now,
its wet mouth licking and tickling you
in its greedy search, its tongue
sampling your salt, your moisture –
just so your creature finds me
in the night, greedy and uncivilized,
seeking, yes, my story and my sustenance,
but also the deep, wet hold of home.

When You Were a Boy

As we lay whispering under stars
you told me how, when you were a boy,
sometimes you were strapped to a raft,
naked, with a beautiful naked woman,
and together you rose and fell,
rose and fell on the wide river, wandering
its way until the noise began to grow,
the water reared up, throwing
the two of you against each other —
not your fault! It couldn't be helped,
and why not take a moment's pleasure
with certain death drawing closer
at every seething bend,
the great falls roaring your name.

How we laughed and, love,
here we are, strapped to a moving raft,
naked as babies in our wrinkled suits.
We are just beginning to gather speed
in the evening light, the rumble of the waterfall
still out of earshot around the last half dozen bends,
a slight vibration in our bodies,
and you can touch me
take me naked in your arms under the oblivious sky
for we know now, no one is watching,
and if anyone eating a sandwich on the shore,
should happen to catch a startled glimpse of us,
our white limbs entangled in sunlight,
I hope they remember our passing
after we're gone.

The Plant Has a Moment of Self-Awareness

Once in a while she awakes
from her dream of their perfect partnership,
the two of them working side by side,
two strong and independent humans,
and sees, in the moment's clarity,
him tending her soil, catches him checking
her leaves tenderly for mites,
murmuring all the while how she is rare,
cherished, and she knows in that moment
that she is a plant.

The only plant in his garden,
she sustains him, provides the fruit,
the very air, he needs to live,
and in return he measures her care
with long and solemn thought,
close attention to the balance
of her temperature control,
adding a little something here for growth,
pruning and shaping by night, the way she likes it,
taking away the old growth
to make way for the new,
and harvesting regularly,
for more and larger blossoms.

And in the seasons of her thriving
now and then she bolts, sends runners
out into the garden, begins to forget him,
to believe she is running the whole garden,
and while his back is turned, suddenly everything
goes to chaos, her ego swelling the fields,
the lawns, obliterating his view.
                                        Calmly

he steps in. Gently he pulls her tentacles
out of the earth, careful to cause no hurt.
She lets go like an obstreperous child,
overtired, relieved to be taken by the hand,
led back to safety and a warm bed.

Carefully he cuts her back to a sustainable
size and shape, frowning with small worries,
and as he works, she grows drowsy, drifts
back into the dream.

CREATION

At the feast of the ego everyone leaves hungry.

Maybe no one likes you.
Maybe your paintings are ugly,
your shoes too big.

Petal after petal you create yourself,
a glowing flower you carry before you in a porcelain bowl
stepping carefully around rocks and trees
placing your bare feet gently among the stones
so as not to tip the bowl, damage the flower.

But what can you do with your own appalling excrement,
your selfish heart beating under the stethoscope?

All of it is make-believe –
children at dress-up.

Give a hand, enjoy
the give and take.
Give your dress away.

Crack the bowl and let the water
seep away. Set it on the shelf.
Let the flower go
the way of flowers.

Prom Queen

One afternoon my slightly grizzled but very trim husband
will drive slowly down the main street of our town
in his sweet gold convertible, its top neatly folded back,
and I, my middle aged flesh molded not-too-tightly
into a silver-blue satin gown, will perch on the back
of the seat wearing long white gloves and a silver sash,
and I'll wave slowly, gracefully to the puzzled tourists
strolling outside the shops, and the busy locals,
many of whom will recognize me, will wave back
in surprise and laughter.
                                    My diamond tiara
from the Dollar Store will glitter in my thinning hair,
and my chubby right arm will move gently,
pushing a breeze in a figure eight: *elbow, elbow,*
wrist, wrist, wrist – my properly cupped hand turning
while my left arm cradles the dozen long-stem red roses
my husband will have nabbed at Albertson's that morning
when he went for coffee.
                            Or maybe
this will never happen,
never need to happen,
and this poem will be enough.

SPILLED HONEY

BROKEN (A RANT)

"Too many things are happening for even big hearts to hold."
            Anne Sexton

Broken hearts, broken bones, broken vows, promises, records,
broken noses, broken dreams, broken arrows, broken
bottles in the alley where the street guy throws his anger,
broken oil tank on the Valdez, broken wings, broken feathers,
black seas, rising seas, broken ice shelf, white bears falling
in the ocean, broken migration routes, swimming bears,
stranded elk, wrong side of the highway, wrong side
of the dam, broken salmon stair, broken fishermen,
dying towns, giving up, giving in, broken immune systems,
cancer cancer cancer, diabetes, new diseases, polyurethane
melting in the sun, give it to the kids to drink, microwave it
into broken eggs, fork them up, broken bird eggs
where the acid rain, broken atoms rushing fusion
reactions long tube blowing, broken watch
throw it in the basket, leave it
with the other trash, buy
another buy another
buy another –

The Answer

(After a long depression, Carter Cooper asked his mother, "Will I ever feel again?" and then jumped from her 14th story balcony.)

How would it be in the moment when his hands,
once the little hands you gave peanut butter sandwiches to,
scrubbed afterward with a yellow washcloth,
when those hands, now rough and bitten, blistered
and sore, gripping the metal railing
let go, disappeared?
                          Absolute silence,
I suppose, or maybe the sound inside the shell
we call the sea, a white noise, the roar
of nothingness just before it enters the heart,
fills it until it overflows with all that nothing,
cannot contain so much empty air and silence,
and then, I suppose there would be screaming
coming from somewhere, sirens, voices would come
and fill the space, hands would take you
by the shoulders, turn you away, tell you where
to put your feet.
                      And you would take up the reins
of your life's journey, but that moment when he hung
there, asked that question, would shine on, I think,
in the dark of your heart, where he had passed it
on to you for safe keeping, and the *no* of it
would keep you hanging forever
from your own balcony, above your own secret
abyss.

The Drought, the Famine, the Vulture
(Kevin Carter defends his Pulitzer-Prize-winning photo)

See the Sudanese child crawling toward
the aid station just outside the frame.
*There is light there is sky there is the life
I am not meant to have.*
                      It keeps on all around:
beetles belly up waiting for the shadow
rabbits screaming in the tall grass, worms half crushed
half drowning. We are swimming in an ocean of half dead
things hanging on, going down
things being eaten alive.
                    How should one man
with a camera change a pattern so vast?
The heart can take in only one death at a time:
and surely the photo itself woke someone up,
saved a hundred lives. Here is the vulture
eyeing the child, hoping for something to eat –
I did walk over and shoo it with my hat –
whether the child perished
I never learned.
                You may forgive me.
Here is the noose, the leather foot stool.
The suffering's too loud.
I cannot hear the rain.

Watching

In this photo: Omayra, trapped in white mudslide,
Armero, Colombia, 1985. Three days and nights
they try to free her, then her heart gives out.
Fournier isn't there; he's mailing his roll of film
home. Held her hand, ran his fingers through
her shiny curls, took her photo. Took it.
Here it is, in this shiny magazine.
                                                    While he watches,
while they all watch, her smile disappears, her voice
loses vigor, becomes a wisp, dark crescents under her eyes
deepen,go black.

Fournier tells himself, sick with guilt,
I am recording her courage
paying tribute to her dignity.

WHAT THE FORTUNE TELLER DOESN'T SAY

I spit on your high-heeled satin boots,
your cultured pearl voice, your
this-is-gonna-be-fuckin-great.
This is gonna be long, is what it's gonna be –
your life. I see it in your eyes:
survivor. But you'll wish it would end
before you're through. No, don't sit down.
I sit. This is *my* world.
You are just passing through,
your keys jingling in your hand,
your eyes cutting to the open door.

There is nothing you can tell me
about bitterness that I haven't bitten off
and swallowed like a bad dream.

But cheer up, honey. There'll be good times.
You'll never be loved, but, honey,
with those boots, you'll be licked up
like sugar on the plate, that hair alone,
that golden dream, will get you in for free
and if you don't mind pawing and drooling
you can pick your fancy furs.

You'll have a few good years
and then your good months here and there
and then, well, you get my drift:
it all comes down to hemorrhoids
and the smell of fried food,
somebody you don't know from Adam
calling you Sweetie
asking you what you want for lunch
like lunch
is gonna make it
all right.

LIFE AFTER
for M.L.
"Everybody sees you're blown apart
Everybody feels the wind blow."
                Paul Simon

A woman comes in and joins us for dinner
at the Mexican restaurant, someone's friend,
a middle-aged beauty with slanted green eyes and pixie hair.
We're a jovial group, but prone to quiet
moments while we listen intently
to the words someone is speaking.

A young man is talking about disciplining children,
how Berkeley people are so crazy
with fear of abuse that they report spanking
to the police, feel free to reprimand mothers
in public for yelling at their kids who are
tearing around in a store
making other shoppers miserable.
When we laugh, she joins in,
throwing her head back, and the shock
of her laughter is so loud, so cold,
sudden and sharp,
that everyone else stops laughing.

And now she speaks up, tells the story
of a man she saw get out of his van
and beat his child with a belt, how she
called the police, but they didn't come
until after the two had driven away
and nothing could be done for the child.

Finishing the story smiling, she
laughs again, inexplicably, that sudden high loud note
scratching at our hearts. Amid murmurs
and head shaking; we begin to pick up our bags,
gather our coats around us.

Leaving the restaurant, someone
holds the door for her. People fall back
and away, avoiding her circle of despair.

But two women who know she has lost a child,
walk close, their hands gently touching
her back, taking her arms, leaning their
warm bodies into hers.

End Game

Not so much death as an end to decision making,
being bright and brittle, embarrassing mistakes,
bald spot at the center when you bow under lights,
the name of the thing you saw, that image
walled up forever in the catacombs
of your mind, and what is that thing,
that bicycle or ghost approaching
from the right?

No one touches you.

Where are the hands, bright words? Stories
you read before sleep, the ones where
you stood up for the underdog,
brave or funny or smart.

What's left is sand and paper in your pockets,
pieces of something stuck between your teeth,
occasional fury, crying in your car. Reduction
continues, a teaspoon at a time, until you're
a watery mess in a chipped brown bowl –
even your taking in and letting out,
no longer a dream machine but
a contraption, too much
of an old thing.

Put it down – cyanide under the tongue or helium
tank and mask – afterward someone to remove
the evidence, make you legal, make you
properly dead, straight and serene,
more whole than in a long, long time
more true.

HONESTY

In the book of Concealment
you hoarded your little secrets,
tiny flames protected in your hands,
slipped in and out of the dark
crowing like a rooster, your chest puffed
with the hubris of all you pretended to be
when really you were mysterious
as smoke, though you spent yourself
trying to read your own signals.

You sat there running your hands over
the satin of your own technique,
the way you held your cards close to your
beating chest, all the while batting
your mental lashes, saying how
you'd never played this game before,
how you needed to know whether four
of a kind beats two pairs, and where could you buy
a diamond in this town?

In the book of Transparency, after heavy losses,
you put all that behind you, got down
to reality, which had begun to surface
like a face emerging in a Polaroid,
a face you recognized from the mirror
but had never seen from that angle.
That terrified expression.

You decided to say everything
right through the door,
pour all the water out

as fast as the pitcher filled,
let the words flow freely
as the thoughts emerged
so that thinking and speech
joined hands before trickery
even arrived.

These days
you never know what
you might say
and whether it's true or
you're just trying it on but
at least the flame is out
in the air where everyone
knows there's fire and
things might burn.

After

He never said white horse, she
heard the deep melodious South, felt
the blue gaze piercing, was pierced
lay down in the long, soft grass,
opened her lips, let her body
rise under his hands, gave up
everything, fell
into the dream
where
one, two, three,
they crashed out the hole where his seed
went in, she called out
his name.

In due time, the story goes,
the kids grew accomplished,
left. There really was
a white steed ... the father
rode above the fray by day
by night, lifted her
out the casement
they flew
her blue nightgown billowing
her thighs burning
for him.

Autumn came as autumn does.

The Arabian goes lame, the man
dismounts, tired and ill.
There is no more flying
and very little tossing in the long
grass. She holds

his spotted hand, she
carries him over the sorrows,
light as bone. She folds
the blue night gown.
She shoots the horse.

DAYLIGHTING STRAWBERRY CREEK
(Berkeley, September)

Like the aspen trees in the golden grove
seem to be tall bouquets of shimmering yellow leaves
in separate silver vases but are really the same tree
rising up from the same system of pushing, pressing,
winding root, blindly moving to water, to light,
we are sprung from the river
that bubbles and curls beneath the surface
of our lives and into which, turning to our beloved
with a sigh, or taking up the pen, the brush,
the flute, we put a line down now and then,
trail a cool finger tip in the current of mystery.

In sunlight we click along the sidewalk in our busy shoes
where builders, in their wisdom, buried creeks
to make a city square and straight and new,
each of us forging ahead along a line from A to B,
forgetting for the moment
the dream or memory of crookedness,
of things that amble, take the low road,
speed up on the downhill slope, and pool
in the loveliest places. Things that come
together, merge and swirl, whisper along
in the night like a lullaby for tired grown-ups:
follow-me   follow-me   follow-me
follow-me-home.

Coming Home

This morning you smelled like fresh wash
drying on the line. I pressed
you to my face
your blue button shirt
the fur of your chest
its center ravine where my cheek
just fits.

        Coming home
in my hiking boots
tired and full of sun, long distances
of hills still behind my eyes
and the piping of gophers
and my long shadow at low sun
across the valley marching down,
arms lifted high and waving back at me
like branches blowing,
                        I see you
standing by the door in blue
and something lifts in my chest,
some song that's been waiting all day
to finish singing.

SOMETHING COMING

We are beginning to understand something
of what is coming, to go beyond sensing a shadow
in the woods watching us, and to see it take shape,
see it coming toward us across a field, zigzagging
as it does, now standing idle and watching the sky,
now heading directly for us at a trot. And realizing
that we are seen, that it will find us no matter
what we do, we are slowing down.
                                    We are
standing very still hoping to blend with the waving
greens of this raw springtime, to stay upwind
of it as warmer breezes pick up and buffet the leaves,
the grasses, tossing everything in a moving salad
of life; we sway on our legs, trying to move with the air
that surrounds us, and we stop thinking of what is around
the next bend in the path, stop planning our next
escape route, and begin to merge with the moment;
we have slipped into a painting by Van Gogh;
something is coming again across the fields and we
are open as sunflowers in full bloom
to these last moments on the earth.

You Notice the Body: Reprise

Notice how, when the air comes in fully, suddenly,
the nostrils close around it, narrowing the passage,
protecting the sinuses, the lungs, the brain,
from a withering blast. Notice
how the hands, clutched together in the lap
begin to tingle, especially the right one
near the ball of the palm, where it goes
numb from time to time, like that nerve
above the right upper lip that receives
the occasional frisson of electrical knowledge.

This is the body now. Not so much
roar of passionate blood, piquant
touch of nipple so exquisite, so sharp
as to be almost intolerable, fingers sinking
into dark warmth almost enough to send
us plunging over the falls in a blue-black wave.

Formless and shapeless now, our pleasure
not so deep, spread out like spilled honey,
a thinner layer of sweetness coming from the skin,
but a thicker strata beneath, roots entwined and matted
all the way down into the water table
where our thoughts drink and swim.

                                    Taste
is the best thing the body does now
on a regular basis, a plump shrimp in cocktail
sauce, a spoonful of home-made cherry
preserves, a bite of cinnamon bread toasted
and melted in butter.
                        But the black veil
of guilt falls over these moments,

grit in the mouth of pleasure, the
sorry hand on the belly folds.

                                      Better
now by far to take up and hold in the inner
eye the silver river, its shores alight
in new minted particles of sunleaf,
the rusted red tricycle in the emerald green
stalks, a wash of yellow flowering trees –
replay all day the last Om at the end
of yoga class – all those voices each
launched forth into the swell of the wave,
all those breaths extended until the rivulets
roll up the beach of silence.

                                Yes. And the Berkeley
air as you drive into the hills, open the window,
your lungs, to the sea and the Mexican orange,
wafting on the balmy breeze.
                                      Notice that.
Commit it to memory for later review,
distant caressing, fondling, shiny coins
in a velvet box.

                        How we begin to love the saving,
the memory becoming almost more than experience
itself. How we store the fragrant lilac,
blue jay in the yellow leaves,
the river music of an hour,
in case we should relive our lives in prison cells,
hospital beds, rocking chairs, blind
or deaf, ill or lost, in case
every sensory miracle
                            should be our last.

THE OTHER BODY

He lies, his head tipped
back on the pillow, eyes closed,
face exposed.
She rattles the tube of gel
touches his forehead,
poor eye socket,
with her cold fingers,
pulls open his lid.

His blue eye is waiting
in its scratchy darkness
for the cool relief
the strip of ointment
laid along the tiny trench
of his pale lashes,
their fragile crescent.

Careful not to touch
the gelatinous pool,
she whispers and, holding
his bony cheek, blots dry
the cracked skin at the corners.

Seven times a day
they perform this ritual
of need and relief.
Sometimes she comes
bare breasted
so their bodies
will have something
nice to do
while his dry and failing
eyes receive these

ministrations of love.
And afterward
often she bends
lays her head
on his warm chest,
checks in with his heart
still thumping
its finite number of bumps
in the dark mystery
of the body she knows
and cannot ever know.

THE TRAIN

There is the hum at 3 a.m. of a passing train
down in the flats, along the Bay,
and the sound carries up to the hills
where a wife lies, not waking,
but dreaming of waking, dreaming
of faces out the windows of trains,
faces in the uncurtained windows
of unpainted shacks, alone with a single bulb
as the train crashes by, full of the lucky ones
who can leave.
                     There is the hum
of that train about to enter the station
as the woman in the burgundy hat
feels the platform vibrate under her Sunday shoes
buttons her coat against the wind ahead
of the train, picks up her brown paper bag
of old letters, yellowed photos, a hand-knitted
scarf, some baby shoes, a Milky Way,
and she waits there
to get on the train.

Gail Rudd Entrekin has an M.A. in English Literature from Ohio State University and has taught poetry and English literature at California colleges for 25 years. Poetry Editor of Hip Pocket Press since 2000, she edits the press' online environmental literary magazine, *Canary* (www.hippocketpress.com/canary).

She edited the poetry & short fiction anthology *Sierra Songs & Descants: Poetry & Prose of the Sierra* (2002) and the poetry anthology *Yuba Flows* (2007).

Her poems have been widely published in anthologies and literary magazines and were finalists for the Pablo Neruda Prize in Poetry from Nimrod International Journal in 2011. She and her husband live in the hills of San Francisco's East Bay.

www.ingramcontent.com/pod-product-compliance
Lightning Source LLC
Chambersburg PA
CBHW032131090426
42743CB00007B/554